Mark Grist is a Peterboroug
and educator with a growir
popular short films on You]

Mark initially grabbed the
a video of him battling teenage grime artist MC Blizzard went viral. The video has since notched up 4 million hits on YouTube, making it the most viewed UK rap battle of all time. Mark has continued to battle a range of MCs from both the UK and overseas, and is currently developing a feature film based upon his rap battle experiences with Shine Media.

In 2013 Mark created a Spoken Word video in partnership with Guy Larsen and The Roundhouse in London called *Girl Who Reads*. The response to the project was unprecedented, with the video gaining over a million views in its first 48 hours. It hit the front pages of Reddit, Buzzfeed, YouTube UK, Huffington Post and UpWorthy.

Mark has performed on BBC Radio 1, BBC Radio 6 Music, BBC2, ITV and BBC3 and taken shows to Denmark, New York and Singapore. He starred in Channel 4's *Mr Drew's School for Boys*, where he developed a range of strategies to engage boys in literacy.

Dan,
I hope
you enjoy
these!

ROGUE TEACHER

MARK GRIST

Illustrated by Guy Larsen

Burning Eye

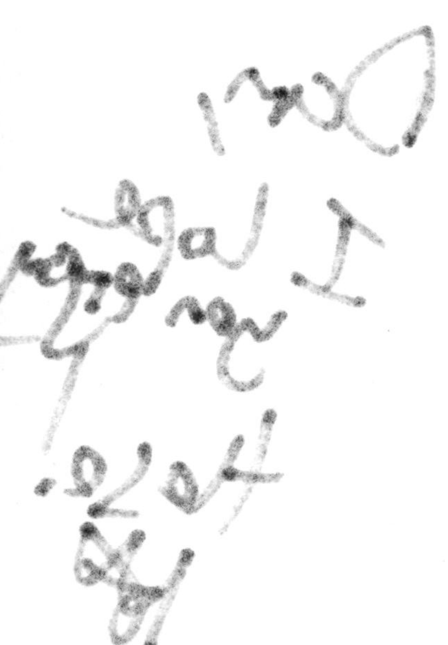

This edition published by Burning Eye Books 2015
www.burningeye.co.uk

@burningeyebooks

Burning Eye Books
15 West Hill, Portishead, BS20 6LG

ISBN 978 1 90913 653 3

For Mum & Dad

CONTENTS

THANKS FOR PURCHASING

May your takeaways stay warm
and your choc-ices stay frozen.
May your kettle have no limescale
and your pipes avoid corrosion.
May every sexual partner
love you beyond devotion.
May your every act be potent.
May your voice now boom like Odin's.

May you tower over others
like a mighty feudal shogun.
May your cereal stay crunchy
after weeks of being open.
May the world now shed a tear
each time you put your clothes on.
May your poo now smell like roll-on.
May you get all the promotions.

May you sprout a set of wings
just because you want to grow them.
May a secret school of wizardry
offer you enrolment.
May any telemarketer
who calls you end up choking.
May your showers not be golden
(unless that's the type you've chosen).

GIRL WHO READS

'So, what do you go for in a girl?'
he asks, lifting the lager to his lips.
Gestures where his mate sits,
then downs his glass.
'He prefers tits. I prefer arse.
What do you go for in a girl?'

I feel a little uncomfortable.
The air left the room a long time ago.
All eyes are on me. Look,
if you must know...

I'd like a girl who reads.
Yeah. Reads.
I'm not trying to call you a chauvinist
and I know you're not alone in this,
but I'd like a girl who reads.
Who needs the written word.
Who uses the added vocabulary
she gleans from novels and poetry
to hold lively conversation
in a range of social situations.

I'd like a girl who reads. Whose heart bleeds
at the words of Graham Greene. Or even Heat magazine.
Who ties back her hair while she's reading Jane Eyre
and who goes cover to cover with each Waterstones three-for-two offer,
but I want a girl who doesn't stop there.

I want a girl who reads.
Who feeds her addiction to fiction with unusual poems and plays
that she hunts out in crooked bookshops for days and days and days.
She'll sit addicted at breakfast, soaking up the back of the cornflakes box,
and the info she gets from what she reads makes her a total fox
'cause she's interesting and unique
and her theories make me go weak at the knees.

I want a girl who reads.
A girl whose eyes will analyse
the menu over dinner.
Who'll use what she learns to kick my arse in arguments
so she always ends the winner.
But she'll still be sweet and she'll still be flirty
'cause she loves the classics and the classics are pretty dirty
and that means late at night she'll always have me in a stupor
as we re-enact the raunchy bits from the works of Jilly Cooper.

See, some guys prefer arses,
some prefer tits,
and I'm not saying that I don't like those bits,
but what's more important,
what supersedes
is a girl with passion, wit and dreams.
So I'd like a girl who reads.

SEX FOOD

Some couples,
when being intimate,
like to cover each other in chocolate.
I heard this can get some couples hot, but
it's not for me.
I prefer my sexual thrills
more savoury.
So when you're done stripping
and dancing wavy,
get over here
and I'll cover you in dumplings and gravy.

A HOME FOR YOUR BOOKS

For Lucy

Well, we got rid of the freezer,
so there's a corner space ready,
and if needs be I'll happily chuck out the telly.
If there's more then we'll store them
on the arms of the sofa,
in the fruit bowl, on the toilet,
in the space for the toaster.
I'll find a home for your books,
any cranny or nook.
If the books
come with you,
then I reckon we're good.

WHAT FROZEN FINGERS NEED

'Ketchup?' said the first cannibal.
'Not ketchup, no,' said Jen.
'Mustard?' said the second.
'Oh, no, mustard tastes awful.' She shivered.
'Then what should we add?' they asked.

'How about you don't add anything?' said Jen.
'How about you don't eat my fingers at all?'

The cannibals looked at each other.
'We are being referenced as first and second cannibal,'
said the first cannibal.
'It would be strange if we didn't eat you,' said the second.
'That doesn't mean anything,' said Jen.
'This isn't really even a poem.
It's just a conversation
that's been given unnecessary line breaks.'

'Fuck you,' said The Poet. And they gobbled her up.

LET US BE STILL

Let us be still, for just a moment.
Let those flames of concern no longer burn
wild in your heaving cage.
Cast it off.
Here, we can dream away our age
and the injustices of our encounters can bound after rabbits,
soft on the breeze.

Let us be still, for just a moment.
Let's forget our mouths and their endless news,
drown our mobiles in the reeds.
Dump our keys
in unbothered grass.
The appointment,
the disappointment can pass.
Allow our eyes to close,
remember ourselves
within each breath.

Let us be still
for just a moment.

Let's you just be you and I'll just be me.
Not those petty rasping things the world
can sometimes make us be.
And the trees, the leaves,
the birds, the bees
will hum above, around, within us

because we are still
and we are free.

CHANNEL 9

What on earth do you think you're all doing?
I can't believe what I see!
To be out here enjoying nature with friends
when you could be inside watching TV!
Did you think that we just wouldn't notice?
Did you think that we'd let it all fly?
After months programming trash
just to make you all laugh,
the odd clip show to watch
while you're running your bath,
those phone-in quizzes
where the prize really goes to our staff.
That was all done for you.
Or at least on your behalf.

And do you consider your actions a victimless crime?
Think 'we can't really watch TV all of the time'?
Well, big mistake!

For we are Channel 9.

We select our execs with much less of a spine.
You'll find we've grown attached
to your fickle attention,
won't give eyes and ears up
without due intervention.

Yes, we've rallied ourselves
in our Channel 9 tower,
scoured the ratings
for hour upon hour,
digested the spreadsheets
in darkened décor,
we've tortured researchers
then tortured some more.
Called in focus groups,
wrapped them tight in barbed wire,
slammed tequila in boardrooms,
chucked kids on the fire.
And when it all seemed quite hopeless,
the foie gras all gone,

a junior executive,
soulless and young,
leaned in and said...
'Do you remember that film in the eighties?
The one with

Kevin Costner?

Where he spent all his time with those Native Americans,
'til he lost his westernised ideals
that stopped him keeping it real,
when he learned from nature how to feel
and hunted for his meals?

Well,
why don't we steal the title of that film,
and use it literally?'

Imagine the slick kick to the public
we'd transmit
if we break all the rules.
If we give them
what they truly deserve,
if we give them...

Celebrity
Dances
With
Wolves.

On ice.

It's a subtle blend of heartwarming
howling and growling
with desperate TV icons
who haven't yet thrown the towel in.
Yes, real celebrities.
Real ravenous wolves.
And real ice.
Yes, real ice.

Every day after school
watch the crusty old act
in the shiny new suit,
the wafer-thin model
in the dress that's minute,
the parade of wolves
who've been starved for a bit,
how long will Keith Chegwin last
'til his jugular's split?

You've got to admit
we've got our hands on a hit
as you pick up the remote with confusion
and sit
and watch
All Of It.

Fear
mixed with our finest canned laughter
as each wolf gets hold
of its dancing partner.
There's confusion and menace,
there's blood and there's sweat.
There's a gnashing of teeth
beneath each pirouette.

And whilst you're absorbed
by those hounds in ball gowns
we'll buy up the green spaces
and burn them all down
so that nothing distracts
from the wolves that are hurled
on ice thin as your link
with the rest of the world.

And you can whine all you like
but the future is here.
Forget family and friends;
they'll soon disappear.
It's a future of nature in tatters,
of Technicolor despots divine.
The future's not yours.
It is ours...
The future is now
Channel 9.

A TEACHER, EH?

The starter's removed.
The main course emerges.
And when I'm asked what I do for a living
our host's reaction verges
on the incredulous.
Half-digested food that's been fed to us
spittoons from his lips.
He leans in, snarls and quips,
'A teacher, eh?
Wouldn't catch me wasting my time
with today's youth.
Just a bunch of grubby little shits!'

The wolves laugh around him,
applaud the wit that he just fired.
His wife smoothes my arm like it's tablecloth,
she says, 'No wonder he looks so tired!'
The room erupts again and I laugh too
because she's right.
I am tired.

I'm tired from days spent
saying, 'Tuck in that shirt.'
From getting kids into lines,
and making girls unroll their skirts.
I'm tired from setting tests
to the grumbling and complaining.
Exams get me stressed.
Giving detentions can be draining.
And who'd have guessed it'd be so tiring
making lessons entertaining?
The kids don't care, 'cause someone's farted
or had a nosebleed
or it's just raining.

And I'm tired from working with artists,
with athletes, with dancers.
I'm tired from asking questions
'til I realise I don't know all the answers,
and then I'm tired from watching the sparks that
fly behind young eyes.

The heroes born in the classroom.
The self-worth they realise.
And then those other kids
where you have to tie on a line,
dive deep inside,
rescue the shreds of confidence
another adult rusted up inside.
I'm tired from scrabbling at those locks,
dredging back those pearls,
then saying, 'Well done, I'll see you next week.'
Letting them back out into the world.
I'm tired of teaching Year 8 boys
that flirting isn't just kicking girls.

And I'm tired of working with young people
who invest in their community
who aren't happy accepting
our grown-up mediocrity.
And while the efforts of the majority sink
to the back of the local paper,
the one kid with a blade who hates the world
because nobody taught him better
gets plastered on page one,
so when I am tired, when our work is all done
I get to stand on duty, watching adults' fearful looks
directed at my young minds, laughing
as they travel home with their books.

But look. Mostly right now I'm tired
because yesterday in class
we were discussing poverty in Uganda.
Throughout it my students were irate,
raw with anger.
They just couldn't understand the fact that young people
are starving in our world by the score.
And when one girl asked me, 'Sir. How can this happen?
How can you adults let the poor stay poor?'

It got me thinking all night about what I once stood for.

So, yeah, you may all be successful.
This meal may well be Michelin.
But I'd swap the swine around me now
for a dozen kids on Ritalin,
'cause those 'grubby little shits'
won't learn your layers of indifference.
And I am tired. I'm exhausted.
But teaching's what I do.
I feed others before I feed myself
so that (fingers crossed)
I never become
as overfed as you.

THE BISCUIT KING

Quick, come to the staffroom!
Leave all your lessons.
There's a magical man
with the greatest intentions.
Throw the books out the window,
let them all disappear.
The rapture's upon us,
the Biscuit King's here!

The Biscuit King's here!
Yes, the Biscuit King's here!
Share the love; bring a mug,
for his words are sincere.
As he pours you your tea,
he struts like a peacock.
Every biscuit on show
that a teacher could dream of.

We'll munch on in wonder,
the young ones, the oldies.
We'll cower and sob
as he lobs Garibaldis.
What a man, what a monster.
We'll gorge upon rich tea.
'Does he long for an assistant?
Oh, please, pick me!' 'No, pick me!'

And we'll each stuff our faces,
we'll weep and applaud him,
then he'll offer us more,
if we do just one more thing.
'That's right, my pretties, more biscuits!'
Some laughter, then,
'That is, if you'll march
on the Houses of Parliament.'

'Oh, yes, Biscuit King!'
we'll scream out with love,
and we'll take to the streets
'til the streets fill with blood.
We'll gut all the leaders;
we'll feast on intestines,
then wash it all down
with Earl Grey and digestives.

The Biscuit King rules!
The Biscuit King rules!
And our heads will be covered in
brandysnap jewels.
We'll dance all around him,
each like a baboon.
For it's biscuits, yes biscuits
that rule the staffroom..

I'VE BEEN THINKING ABOUT DEATH A LOT

And why not? It seems like a massive theme.
It's huge, with power. Actually,
there's no theme greater, or more torturous,
the one thing in life guaranteed to strike all of us.
And a lot of writers try to scribble thoughts
on death, but once dead you don't come back,
so we can't write work that's been informed,
which means a lot of it is pretty crap.
Well, why stop now? Yes, here's my try:
I've decided I'm not going to die.

I mean, come on, it seems rubbish, right?
Why pass on to the other side?
Why pay the price for tons of crimes
that even now don't come to mind?
Or what if it's eternal sleep?
That's pretty disappointing.
For the rest of time? Seems pretty cheap.
I don't think I'd enjoy it.
I don't want some endless slumber time.
I'm loving life, why stop the ride?
You know what? I won't compromise.
I tell you, I'm not going to die.

I'll build a fortune, slowly growing,
with pennies that I made from poems.
Pennies to be mostly spent on
scientists, experiments from
noon to nightfall, smoothing, making
fresher organs, teeth that gleam.
Bit by bit rejuvenating
every single piece of me,
and my minions may wonder why
I won't join that deathly conga line.
Screw them, I won't be undermined!
I tell you, I'm not going to die.

I'll make them work throughout the night
On backups for the human mind.
Moisturiser layered upon me,

nutrients into the bloodstream,
fountains of youth
to keep me hydrated,
refusing to move
so muscles aren't ageing.
Nothing to do, but it's pretty great, 'cause
while the others I knew
are slowly erased
I'll last in the dark,
my laughter sublime,
deep in these sarcophagi.
Just me, just me
and loads of brine.
I tell you, I'm not going to die..

And you might be thinking
that'll never happen or *he's a little egocentric.*
Maybe, yeah, but I'd do it.
I'm really scared to end this.
I'm terrified, lie awake at night,
can't get out of my head
how short the time we spend alive,
how long we'll end up dead.
Even this piece I'm writing now
is more likely to be seen after I've died.
So any meaning I could assign feels in itself a waste of time.

Look,
I guess,
if you do discover this piece
in a cupboard somewhere or posted up online,
just know there was a guy who was once alive
who wasted a day on some rambling
rhyme
about how much,
how much
he really doesn't want to die.

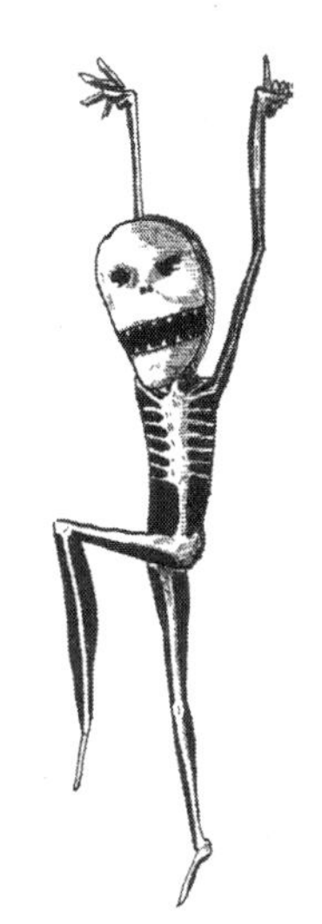

LUMP

Before we knew each other
I was lump,
a restless clump of energy,
eager to blunder through the world.

In those early years we sank
together in your armchair.
Me, a clay ball
on your lap turning pages,

tracing fingers as you read to me;
filling my head with the actions
that make us worthwhile.

I climbed the gate for that girl at nursery,
told Ryan Skuse to leave them alone
until he thumped me in the mud.
And I was slippery with tears,

until I was in sight of you.

Now my heart gulps
as you tell me
about this new lump,
cold lump, uninvited

and you cry down the phone
and later so do I
at the lump in my throat
lump in my throat

that just won't go away.

THE HISTORY AIN'T BRIGHT, THE HISTORY'S MISS KNOWLES

For Ericha

I'm here to warn you all
of a teacher in our school.
She's more foul than Simon Cowell
and a dozen times more cruel.
She's a schemer, a despot,
a crafty cardboard cut-out captor.
Feasts on the fear of first-years
like some blonde velociraptor.
And she'll slap ya with a warning
almost each and every morning
for saying 'hi' or yawning
any time that you walk past her.
Nothing faster on two legs
within the corridor she patrols.
The history ain't bright,
the history's Miss Knowles.

And for five days every week,
her form group shuffle into class
hoping she won't get competitive
over another inter-form task.
As she settles on her throne,
her potent voice will ask,
'Who'll help me win the sports day?
Second place is as good as last!'
If the homework comes in late
her eyes grow dark and smoky.
Shares a surname with Beyoncé,
but she's crap at karaoke.
And woe betide you if you're jokey,
woe betide you if you're giggling.
Forget Snape from Harry Potter;
she's the perfect Head of Slytherin.
A raise of brow, a lift of head
and half the class start piddling.
Impaling those she catches fiddling
on the heels from off her soles.
The history ain't bright,
the history's Miss Knowles.

That's right, the history ain't bright,
the history's Miss Knowles.
She fills her drawers with tights
in case the ones she wears get holes
and along with the scent of brimstone
that pervades throughout her room,
lunchtime sushi fills the air
almost every afternoon.
While she sits in her free periods,
she marks and thinks and swoons,
imagines Jeremy Paxman
would visit her in her room.
And you are doomed
if you dare
to distract from this immersion.
She's got a huge set of lungs
for such a little person.
Don't go in there, try reversing.
Hurry! Quickly!
Save your souls!
The history ain't bright,
the history's Miss Knowles.

STILL THE KIDS DON'T GIVE A SHIT

You try to plan for everything.
You smile each day you let 'em in.
You tell them they're intelligent,
and still the kids don't give a shit.

So you head away, reflecting that
you'll fix it in your lesson plans,
no filler, no digressions and
yet still the kids don't give a shit.

You start to worry, ask for help.
You take on the advice,
replay days they weren't engaged
in fitful dreams throughout the night.
Your weekends are mostly spent
applying words of wisdom
to lesson plans longer
than Apple's terms and conditions.

And you make displays, start laminating,
apply for extra IT training,
hours at the copier waiting.
Still the kids don't give a shit.

That roleplay that you thought was fun,
that really moving scene that's from
that sitcom that you loved when young:
well, still the kids don't give a shit.

You purchase books with stocky headings,
try to make sure fun's embedded,
differentiate your questions,
chuck in the odd *TOWIE* reference,
coax them out of disagreements,
celebrate each small achievement,
pin their work from floor to ceiling,
but each week you can't believe it.
Nothing changes, nothing shifts.
Not one piece of info sticks
'til deep inside you something flips.
You turn and say, 'Right, listen, kids,

'I've spent whole terms amassing failure.
I've been warden fused with entertainer,
chat show host, lion tamer,
farting scissors, shitting paper.
I never leave my kitchen table,
I've got glitter purchased by the spadeful,
Fucking hours in fucking Staples!
Still nobody gives a shit.

I studied this, I worked for ages
for glassy stares from dull teenagers,
I could throw a hand grenade
but none of you would give a shit!'
And they'll sit there silent; stare right back

while pain shoots up, your knees go slack.
It seems you're having a heart attack
And still the kids don't give a shit.

But what's that falling from your pocket?
A little, wrapped-up piece of chocolate.
My, look, how they all stare upon it!
Oh shit, oh shit, they give a shit!

'It's OK, guys! Don't call for help.
Just work through questions 6 'til 12.
This goes to whoever does it well.'
Oh shit, oh shit, they give a shit!

'While you do that, I'll just lie down.
I feel a little tired now.
But carry on; please don't slow down.
You know what? I feel really proud.'

NUTMEG

As a teenager, I was called a 'jitter' in my hometown.
Now, jitters were guys who were renowned for our frowns,
and our interest in the post-grunge sound.
With dyed hair and purple DMs bound tight
below shredded jeans and rock T-shirts,
we thought we looked all right,
and we found that looking alternative could get the girls
a little flustered.
It was something that was to prove very popular for Busted.

So we cultivated a look similar to the modern-day emo, just more
well-adjusted
and with brighter clothes:
Reading Festival bands the colour of mustard
and those black studded gloves.
We looked dangerous and morose,
being followed by security as we moped about in Waitrose.
And whilst sipping on cider
or going through roll-ups
we sat at the swings and moaned about grown-ups
and we talked about girls and the bands that we liked, and the
plethora of heavier drugs we should try.

Because we'd all seen TV, we all read *Kerrang!*,
to us, music and drugs sort of went hand in hand.
Every artist we rated celebrated their blazing
on festival stages, or else raged against 'em
in interview statements, complained how it aged 'em.
Even that sounded great; we just wanted a way in.
And this was frustrating, like some really bad joke.
The dealers round our way were nastier blokes,
ravers in puffer jackets;
you'd get smashed to a pulp
if you, as a jitter, tried blagging some dope.
And so each night we talked highs,
just how much we lusted
for some kind of drug.
Until Chen mentioned nutmeg.

That's right. Nutmeg's a drug.
He printed off from the 'net
details of its psychedelic effects,
plus a comment that one trip was 'better than sex'.
I have to confess
we were pretty impressed,
as guys who hadn't tried either of those yet.
And we scavenged our spice racks,
sidestepped our mothers,
scooped up supplies,
met with each other,
pooled our resources,
grated the lot,
filled empty bottles of Robinsons squash
with powder, used water to top it all up.
We did up the lids and swiftly took off.

And we went to The Witches
and sat on the stump.
We opened the bottles. Fuck, did they hum,
but we weren't giving up on what we'd begun.
Held noses to thumbs, proceeded to chug
for about thirty seconds,
then began to throw up.

A lot.

And as we threw up, we staggered and roared,
spewing chunks of nutmeg on us all,
finally each lying gripped to the floor,
heaving to the point we couldn't heave any more.
And whilst we were there,
we spluttered and chatted
of how we might die,
our faces all plastered
in each other's vomit,
that nutmeg and acid.
It felt like an age, but just two hours had passed
and then it wore off.

We washed in the river
and each headed home
to safety and dinner.

I'm a lot older now and I don't want to spoil it
with too many details;
I've hugged a few toilets.
I'm aware of the hard stuff, I choose to avoid it.
I still drink and I smoke and I mostly enjoy it.
My friends have grown too; some have moved on to better things,
have serious jobs and yet they've done everything.
Some won't touch booze,
one won't take medicine,
and some are a mess
from the way drugs have messed with them.
I saw one the other day; he said he'd give anything
to go back to the point where only nutmeg had tested him.

TROLLING

Everybody's angry
because somebody said something.
They went and said a dumb thing
and stuck it on a blog.

Now half of the web is raving,
there's a ton of scathing statements,
everybody's favouriting
and liking it a lot.

The dramatic escalation
of everything that's pasted
means several back the statement
that triggered it all off.

They snap at those who've spoken up,
say their posts are mostly dumb,
that they are too for posting 'em,
and still the hours plod.

By now we're all invested.
We call each other dickhead.
Each argument's dissected
while sat upon the bog.

We're caught up in the backlash
of vitriol and hashtags,
friends and families tagged back
'til everybody's flogged.

And finally it all implodes.
We take our friends list, trim them so.
We're all agreed, 'we're winners!' Gloat,
'We raised awareness, changed the mob!'

But in each post a mantra sings,
'This really won't change anything.'
'No, this really won't change anything.'
We're typing that a lot.

OGRE

You kept us in check all right, hugged us
with a thuggery unrivalled on our street.
Your bellow from the doorstep, dragging
back to the fortress,
    where you'd lurch through our doorways,
knuckling at dusters; rubbing spit upon faces;
tormenting the dishes;
    you were clatter;
    the business,
    and if one of us resisted
just one glance from you
    lifted the spines off our backs.

One afternoon, while you slept, I crept closer.
Ran my fingers along the red scar in your side,
the one that I'd made.
    Deep as the Earth's crust,
but still nowhere deep enough to be the end of you.

CALMING INFLUENCE

We used to be fast-flowing back then;
the corridor was awash with kids.
Our walls rippled with their thoughts.
The stairwell streamed imagination,
among the roar of their depth,
within the tide of their questions.
And I loved it back then,
but then
you came.

And we settled with you.
Grew a skin around ourselves where the water could be held,
where it could get easier
to manage the flow.
We all knew that it'd stink
but somehow, your voice rose,
channelling the 'idiots', the 'useless',
the 'fuckwits', the 'waste',
'til the tide stopped completely
and the corridor grew flat.

It's been a year now.
I drifted past your room yesterday,
saw, through the bubble of your window,
my kids,
gnashing like a bunch of conned piranhas,
desperate for something to swim in,
whilst you sat in the deepest spot of your room
looking at your pay slip,
as though you'd just earned something.

WHY I'M ANGRY

It isn't that she was rude,
or the detention that she missed,
or the list of obscenities she's hurled at other students,
or that when challenged on her earrings she refuses to remove them.
It isn't that she doesn't understand the poems
or that she wants it all answered for her.
It's not her lack of homework, or her lost report
or that she says things before she's thought them through.
It isn't that she's alone.
It isn't her mascara.
It isn't that the hard kids avoid her
because they think that she's much harder.
It isn't that she caused a riot in my class
by singing the praises of the BNP.
It isn't that she says she hates our school.
It isn't that she questions me.
It isn't that she threw her book on the floor
or that I've seen her cry more than any student I've worked with
before.

It isn't her folder.
It isn't the swastika
or that she smokes behind Tesco when other kids are having dinner.
It isn't that she's often late to my lessons
or the display that she cut up
or that when I asked her why she did it, she said,
'Because I'm a fuck-up, Sir.
Don't waste your time on me, Sir.
Just leave it. I'll never ever get it, Sir.'
It's none of that.

What it is
is that whilst I'm working out
what to try next
to make that poem make sense to her,
to show her that she can do it,
you're sat opposite,
shovelling jelly and ice cream into your face,
scowling as she stomps past,
telling me how you taught her last year,

how you put her in her place,
and that she's 'a fuck-up.
A waste of time. Best to leave her.
She'll never ever get it.'

It's that I've realised what you've been doing.
It's that I've realised what you've done.

It's that you'll only do something if it isn't demanding,
you'll only help the students who won't make a stir,
and whilst you're labelling someone without any understanding
I can see the monster in you that's being made out of her.

BY NUMBERS

For the AQA Chief Examiner, who told my students that 'any poem turned on its side looks like nothing more than a poem turned on its side.'

You'll make the grade, all right: A Vaccination.
Your mother bought you the revision guide.
Well done. Now just hide your mind and slide
towards the exam in June. It's easy for you, laugh
at the back of the room. Because the world can be
a science and doesn't this feel like we're working? Let's just skate the surface. Grow sick of it
together. Enjambment. Personify. Onomatopoeia. Your predictions will always catch you, so
never shake the tree. Only eat the sour stuff, don't think to question me. One day you'll head
off to the right university. Divide yourself further
from the quiet giants you mocked in the corridor.
The herbivores you leapt over in class. Benchmarks
of failure. Darwin's lost hopes. Who got poetry
all wrong. Who wouldn't learn how to pass.

RURAL HACK

He gathered the animals he'd seen that day
around him. Held them in his arms,
promised to take good care with his pen.

Then he stroked them smooth,
lopped off boils and hair,
hugged wrinkles away,
dipped his nib into eye sockets,
split hooves and milky guts.
Pigs squealed the way
you suppose that they should.

Once finished,
he placed them on the page,
a lot like living things
you'd see on a farm.
Their smiles centred nicely,
they stood there, upright,
bound tight in a rhyme
to help keep them all calm.

BETH BUILDER

When I was ten years old I knew her name was alliterative,
but that's not why she gave me thrills
running past the classroom windowsill,
a short skirt, a shrill shriek whenever she ran home from school.
Beth Builder was gorgeous in a way
that you just couldn't score it;
she had beauty in the way that Tony Hart would draw it.
And the primary school rumour mill
was green and in full grind
because Beth Builder had said that she fancied me.
She'd told Liz Windell behind the Cadbury's factory.
It was only a matter of time until she
would maybe, even,
chat to me.

I'd blushed at her company for weeks
and as Liz recounted Beth's speech of fancy
I felt resplendent, my cheeks aflame.
I was reeling during break time
thinking, *Beth Builder feels the same!*
When I went home that night to play my computer games,
she was every princess that I rescued;
I was each hero she did tame.

But in the following days I began to grow dismayed.
See, Beth didn't come and talk to me.
She stayed with her mates, she played by the gates
and when I waved she laughed,
causing my heart to deflate.
As my mates pushed me over,
with an impending sense of dread,
her voice of tender glass cried out,
'Piss off, Cabbage Head!'

Back then my hair was crap and unruly
and during primary school she
didn't want to know me 'cause of all these curls.
And so that whirl of pride that Liz's lies had unfurled
blew up inside
and I began to realise

that love was way more complicated
than I'd been led to understand.
If I was going to go out with Beth Builder
what I needed was a plan.

So I devised one,
using my mother as a template for all women across the land,
but I was so absorbed in my plan, I didn't see or understand
that Beth didn't really care about the English and Maths work
my mother thought was so grand.
Beth Builder's main hobby was preserving dolls in little plastic bags,
while I stuck around for chess club,
Panini stickers and *White Dwarf* mags,
and the fact that Miss Howl's face sagged
when Beth handed in her work:
it just didn't register.
I wanted so badly to impress her, that's the stupor I was in,
that I read like a demon, blazed through the blue, green, red and purple sections
until I was the first kid allowed to read
anything in my school.
And I worked
and worked
and worked

while Beth played, laughed, running round with other boys,
playing stringy onions
and I realised that impressing her with hard work
was probably just nonsense.

So one week, after coming top in some tests,
I thought it might be best to phone Beth Builder and ask her out.
So I did, the receiver slipping in my palms.
When Beth picked up I said, 'Hi,' in a tone that I hoped sounded calm.
She said, 'Who's that?'
I said, 'Um... it's Mark.'
She said, 'Urgh! What, Cabbage Head?'
Here I attempted a feeble laugh.
She said, 'Hang on,' and left for what seemed like ages.
Until another voice came back,
a little gurgling whisper,

and I realised that Beth had put me on the phone
to her little baby sister.
I said, 'Hello?'
A pause, a hesitation, and then a babyish declaration:
'CAB... BAGE... HEAD.'

She'd taught her baby sister to say it.
And I don't know why, but those words
had a kind of scalpel effect on me;
I dropped the phone to Beth's laughter;
ran; tripped on the directory.
Apparently, it was the first time that baby
had said two words consecutively.
But I didn't care.
I'd offered her my heart.
She'd taken all that I was and ripped it apart.
And I promised myself
that I would forever walk the path
that had no girls, no holding hands,
forever and ever and ever and ever.
But I got over it.
And now I'm a teacher and writer and I'm happy with both.
And I thought I'd done pretty well with the scope
of ability at my control.
But even so, something within me stirs at the thought of Beth
Builder.
And I figured maybe it'd be the perfect ending
to this poem if nowadays she had a job that she hated in a shop,
if she cleaned the chicken ovens in Tesco
or mopped people's sick up.
I bumped into her brother Tom and I asked what she was up to.
It turns out that she's now an image consultant in London,
and she's very successful,
and as much as I may hate it I'm kind of impressed. Well,
for the person she was in school, that profession seems great.

And maybe it's not the moments you love,
but more the moments you hate
that make you who you are.
Not just the times you got picked for the team
but more the times you didn't measure up by far.

I think that's why Beth Builder is important.
When I look back and see pictures of the boy who
hadn't met her yet,
who didn't know what he'd grow up to be,
because I think my hair gave Beth Builder her first shot
at image consultancy.
And a bit of the man I am today, she definitely gave to me.

THE FENS

A story with only one vowel

Meet Beth. Twenty-three.
Excellent dresser.
She reeks style.

Weekends, Beth gets cheeky.
Necks WKD recklessly.
She never expected the sheer hell reserved
when she entered the fens.

Ten-twenty
Beth left Ely,
sped her VW Beetle west,
swerved,
    screeched her steed,
beep-beeped the steer wheel.

Her geezer, Stephen, peers meekly.
He resembles Lenny Henry, except he's weedy:
sheep pressed between Spencer's vest.
Beth yells,
    'We'll see the fens, then get wed!'
Stephen remembers the decree.
Keen, he enters the Beetle.
Delves gently, seeks the belt.
Beth revs; they cheer, then speed freely.

When they enter the fens, green fresh smells meet Beth's senses.
Creeks, trees, weeds, levees greet them sweetly.
    Speechless, they creep.
The elements stem themselves,
bend themselves everywhere they step, except
every step gets denser.
The empty greenery seems endless.

Stephen feels creeped.
He pretends the scheme's serene,
    yet every tree leers.
Endless, eyeless, the enemy peers.

Stephen's nerves melt, jelly-blended.
He regrets he needs the strength,
the steel we reserve when we remember
Pelé.

Then, when the deep sky speckles, Beth preps her reedy bed.
Stephen shelters level.
Edgy sleeve tenderly pets Beth's flesh.
Well! Beth's eyes needle
    when she sees the tent he's erected.
Leery breed needs rejected,
Stephen sleeps neglected.

Then, sleep spent, they peel themselves free.
    They creep.
Trees bleed, scenery ferments, Beth tells herself
they'll never flee the fens.

Except: ten weeks spent, Beth emerges.
She enters the next settlement.
Teeters, her energy levels receded.
Her dress shredded, feet wet,
perm demented,
yet she's free.

Yet where's Stephen?

Well, let's expel the mystery.
Heed Beth's well-fed belches, her greedy belly swelled.
She fended when needs expected.
When she felt empty
her Stephen merely resembled
beefy
yet nerdy
entrée.

The end

TERRY AND TIARA

Terry worked in finance.
Tiara did PR.
They'd built up in the city
like a build-up of catarrh,
'cause Terry was obnoxious;
Tiara was the same.
Terry always paid the bill.
Tiara chugged champagne.
And Terry sometimes got too loud
but the service was to blame.
And Terry lived to lie and cheat.
And Tiara weren't her name.

It was really Deborah,
but growing up Deborah had found
that you aren't just you,
you're what you choose to project,
and Deborah had been a name that
so many would forget.
But they wouldn't forget 'Tiara'
with a man on her arm,
a handbag from Prada,
the leggings, the lashes,
the shoes, the car or
enough gold to weigh down
the Spanish Armada.

And Terry was perfect.
He had... good teeth.
Some basic business acumen.
Those depths of human nature?
He was also kind of lacking 'em.
While he had no friends to speak of
(he'd spent December sacking 'em),
he was wealthy. He was on track
like a brown-haired Mika Häkkinen.
And so Terry and Tiara made pretty good partners.
They belched and they bantered
in equal measure.

They scoffed at the meek,
they hoarded their treasure.
They lived it up high
held high in regard
and they lived
and they worked
and they hid
and they fucked
really fucking hard.

And so one night on his chaise longue
cut from rich exquisite leather
Tiara said to Terry,
'We can still do so much better.'
He felt it: a connection
they knew how best to get things
and so Terry, drunk on sherry,
knelt down and popped the question.
Tiara, of course, said, 'Yes!'
Ordered invites to the wedding
Along with huge gift brochures
with some really meaty headings.

Now this was the moment half the city had been dreading.
So what if they did your head in?
You still have to make a good impression.
This invite had them stressing.
One question clutched intestines.
This couple had, well, they had everything.
What on earth would someone get them?

On the day of the wedding the reception seemed vast,
like the party in Carlito's Way had been recast.
A little less cocaine, a little more sea bass.
It was actually pretty cool if you believed all the feedback.
And so Terry and Tiara set off on a honeymoon,
took photos on beaches. After a month they flew
back to their cottage, complete with a stunning view,
and dealt with the presents guests had bought them
to rummage through.

There were tons of them waiting,
stacked wall to wall,
and so throughout the morning
they settled to trawling
through what guests had bought,
finding places to store all
the blankets, fruit baskets, tablets, tie racks,
the balsamic carafes, tablemats made of matchstick,
enough glasses packed they could handle a banquet,
all unwrapped and stacked 'til they filled up the hamlet.

By lunch they were knackered, but the boxes hadn't dwindled.
There were mops, drapes and Kindles,
odd-flavoured tipples,
cross-trainers, little containers for pickles,
and locked in the middle,
light blocked from the window,
they started to wonder just what they'd got into.

They headed to bed. Things covered the floor.
Woke the next day to delivery horns.
Looked out the window, saw sprawled on the lawn
More boxes, more boxes on top of each box.
They dragged them inside 'til they toppled and dropped.
By breakfast the mess was up to their legs, by lunchtime their chests,
by dinner their necks,
'til neither could move and so that's how they slept.

The next day more gifts came, the exits all blocked off.
The cottage was full 'til the roof nearly popped off,
and Terry and Tiara were held and held fast,
all stodged up and blocked and stuffed with their crap.
Inside those things, now breathing her last
Something in Tiara finally cracked.

Slowly,
very quietly,
from the smallest of gaps,
you could hear as she cried,
'Please! Send it all back!'
The delivery drivers, much to their relief,
shrugged and yanked out the gifts piece by piece.

Their heads were freed up; they were able to breathe.
'Take more back!' she shouted and Terry agreed.
They relished their breathing continued the heaving,
'til slowly the pair of them sank from the ceiling.
Each thing they chucked out seemed way less appealing.

Day one, they were smiling.
Day two, they were beaming.
Day three, they felt woozy.
The cottage was roomy.
But they kept up the purge,
continued removing the old stuff they had,
chucked out the plasma,
chucked out Tiara's old handbags and jewellery,
chucked out the sofas,
chucked out the sink,
kept chucking stuff out 'til there wasn't a thing,
just them and some bricks
and as they stood there amidst
this field full of shit, Tiara said
'I think something's wrong with the way that we think.'

It's as though we've been tricked,
or as though we've been sick.
We're wasting our lives stocking up to the rafters
with this tat and that crap.
Look, my name's not Tiara...
I'm Deborah,'
she said,
and Terry's eyes widened.
He looked down at his feet as she stood there beside him.
Then he lifted his head and whispered quite quiet,
'My name isn't Terry. I'm really called Brian.'

And so Deborah and Brian both stood there in silence.
They looked at the items they'd filled up their life with,
the craving for status that's fostered inside us.
It was awful, appalling, they felt sick inside, but
there was something else too, and they couldn't help smiling.

KEITH

Each writer I know has a mind that's polluted
with voices that tell them their work is all useless.
A virus inside them that thrives on defeat.
But they couldn't stop one man, a man they called
Keith.
Now, Keith was a poet; at least he wrote every month
and he read what he wrote, although most of it stunk.
It was turgid at best; every word as it left
would just twirl in the air like a turd in a dress.

And you'd think that with Keith, that voice that's inside him
would have beefed up somewhat, a critical Viking.
That wasn't the case, though. See, Keith wasn't frightened.
He weren't a great writer; he just really liked writing.
So each month in the bar with the mic in the corner
they'd slump as he started reciting this torture.
Dishing out words like a toilet that's blocked,
the images shitty, the rhymes badly forced,
and although they'd dread it every week he still read it,
pulling metaphors like teeth without any anaesthetic.
It was painful all right, but while his work offered no joy,
it did worse than that; it pissed off the old boys.

Because Keith was well known and his name was like venom
to the old boys, who moaned that he just didn't get it.
'What is he doing? Where is the elegance?
Why bother trying? It seems hardly Tennyson!'
This well-trudged routine had gone on for ages,
but one evening Keith brought out a handful of pages.
He started to read and the room became flat
because even for Keith what Keith read was quite bad,
and the old boys all stared, they watched on in silence.
It was bad, really bad. Something grew up inside them.
They started to shake as though channelling demons.
'It's just rhymes!' shuddered one. 'Dear God, there's no reason!'

That night they sat round; dissected the problem.
Keith's work was so bad that they had to do something.
'But what? I mean, what? Nothing's stopping this guy.
You can't put him off by just rolling your eyes
or refusing to clap at the end of recital.'

It would take more resolve, it would take something final.
So they agreed on a plan in the depths of their cloister.
There was only one option.
That option
was
'moider'.

At the next open-mic Keith started reciting.
The old boys were armed, huge bags stacked behind them.
He started his piece and as he hit his stride
their arms darted down, clasped round what's inside,
and in seconds they set to removing his grin.
The tomatoes they threw weren't removed
from no tin.
It was a shocking amount to take on the chin,
on the shin, the shoulder, the temple, the teeth,
the cans hammered hard, he collapsed in a heap
and the old boys all cheered with each thud on his flesh,
and the cans they piled up until poor Keith was dead.

The following day, they stood at his funeral.
One read a piece; it was really quite beautiful
and there in the light it seemed right, all this judgement.
Who best to shield words but those longest incumbent?
They'd pull out the weeds, stop new ones from growing.
Yes, poetry's a standard in need of upholding.

So each month they held cans throughout everyone's work
and they pelted each poet whose poems were worst,
and with those going on facing death on the mic
twenty poets became twelve, became eight, became five.
With the numbers soon dwindling, no newbies to bludgeon,
the old boys in time had to turn on each other.
One night one of them messed up a stanza,
Before he could argue they threw home the cans and
another, one evening, as he went to his kitchen
was greeted with, 'James, your work has been slipping.'
Just another one dead,
another one dead.
Every fudged line meant a can to the head

until finally, one day there was just one poet left
and the standard was high, from start through to finish,
though the open-mic lasted a handful of minutes.
But he didn't feel bad, no weight of the murder,
the blood on his hands; he thought, *I'll go a stage further!*
Why give up on this mighty work we've begun?
Why have all of my poems when you need only one?
Yes, one single poem! Surely that is the answer.
No way anything could lower that standard.

And he laughed to himself as he knew that he meant it,
went home, burnt his pieces; the purge was intensive.
Then standing in front of a mirror quite pensive
he brained himself hard 'til his head was indented,
and that was, well, that;
poetry was safe
and removed from all failings and lofty and great
and lonely and empty and lacking in meaning,
removed from us sinners to rot on the ceiling.

And I wonder sometimes if that's what we're craving
when I see and hear artists obsessed with their slating,
'cause hating each other seems dumb and I'm guessing
we'd stop if we saw down the route that we're heading.

I say here's to each poet who's messed up a piece,
who fucks their work up and still doesn't retreat.
If you ask me, if we're craving more Tennysons and Keats,
it's just as important we cheer on the Keiths.

TRISTAN

'One day, when you're grown up
you'll be a weasel.
All the best little owls grow up to be weasels,'
said Tristan's mother: herself killed and dragged
off by a weasel on her sixtieth birthday.

This encouragement was enough to get him started.
Tristan worked on his bounding,
referred to his feathers as fur,
even kept away from the more 'owly' crowd
to focus on his burrowing.

Each morning he checked his reflection,
but with no success. *What's wrong with me?*
he thought, as he sat beneath the trees.
'You're a very handsome owl,' he was told once,
and it stang like his Mother's cries. Gnawed on his insides
whilst other owls made use of their wings in the moonlight.

ALCHEMIST

One night, believing myself big enough,
I crept out of bed to neck my father's mouthwash.

The mixture burnt my throat,
leapt from mouth and nose
as the bottle dropped:
upended across the lino.

I fell too; scooped with my fingers,
desperate for a solution,
until, none coming and
with the morning fast approaching,
I reclaimed the bottle,
stuffed soap,
toothpaste, water,
shampoo, moisturiser, Calpol,
and bleach inside.
Then I shook it 'til it settled
almost exactly like before.

Later, as I lay awake in my bed
I knew when my father drank it
he'd drop down dead.
And knowing the smack I would get
for owning up,
still I made no sound;

just welled in the dark
at the mixture I was,
so badly diluted
when held up against him.

SMALL TOWN DRAMA

At first, no one knew why the pub was closed,
but drama spread like mustard in our small town.
And so, by the time the doors reopened
local lips were sealed tight
with the three-day-old squeals
we'd heard about at midnight.
The bleating kids clutching their rucksacks tight,
while Mike from the bike shop
had lifted the boot up.
Told the landlord it was over,
he'd been keeping her cooped up,
and she'd squawked in the headlights,
flapped amidst her flight.
Her shrill voice had insisted she was tired of this life.
Tired of all the fights. Tired of telling lies.
And so her tyres told the truth across the tarmac out of sight.

And so, returning to the bar we were all just so surprised
to see John still there. Shirt ironed. His smile firm in place.
Chuckling over frothing pints; contentment on his face
With those eyebrows and cheeks shaking
you could have been mistaken for thinking he was happy.

Except
this huge wall display of olives that had always been behind him
was now gone.
These green and black jars that'd dominated the bar space,
where she'd swooped in, replaced the scratchings, pickled eggs
and uncouth snacks with olives instead.
Now those jars were sacked from the back bar,
and although we heard he'd said nothing
as she drove off in that car,
in the calmness of his surrender
the olives had been his only scalp.
He'd ripped 'em out. Let out one last desperate masculine shout
by replacing them

with pork pies.

And like some corkscrew crusade of a desperate vessel
he sank safe within that fort of brown crusty testicles.
And so he did seem the same
but for those fatty sentries sat
watching him wish for those long lost years back.
And he never ever grumbled,
never once mentioned the kids.
But every Friday, when he'd offer us a pie to go with our pint,
we'd stop laughing.
And for a moment, nothing was as weighty
as the welt of pain on his neck
that he'd sloppily bandaged with gelatine and pastry.

COME TO PETERBOROUGH

Come to Peterborough,
a city of unusual beauty,
houses so cheap
we don't pay stamp duty.
Our team may be called the Posh
but believe me, they ain't snooty,
'cause they still head out to Liquid
when they want to shake some booty.

Come to Peterborough,
the birthplace of George Alcock, MBE.
We're one of four environmental cities
thanks to our greenery.
You can eat out at Nando's,
take in a play at the Key
and enjoy the slightly sexist writing
in a copy of our *ESP*.

Come to Peterborough,
for romantic nights at the dog track,
or walks in Southey Wood.
We don't have a university,
though we know we probably should.
The connecting trains to London
are really pretty good,
although our multi-coloured bin system
is poorly understood.

Come to Peterborough,
and see Longthorpe Tower.
It's protected by law.
Why have one local radio station
when you can have four?
The Regional College doesn't offer A levels anymore,
and we've an IKEA distribution centre
but no fucking store.

Come to Peterborough.
Let the *Evening Telegraph's* reporting
fill you with apprehension.
Revel in the barbs of our racial tension.
Our wide array of pound shops,
oh, they do deserve a mention.
The shopping centre ain't big enough
but we're building an extension.

Come to Peterborough.
We're consistent in our rate of violent crime.
The cathedral looks amazing
when it's bathed in the sunshine.
So what if our manufacturing is currently in decline?

Come to Peterborough.

Please.

Come to Peterborough.
It ain't always a pretty city
but it's mine.

IN DEFENCE OF PUGS

Some people say she's not a proper dog,
and, I don't know, perhaps they're right.
When it came the time to choose a dog,
she wasn't what I had in mind.
I thought we'd get a massive dog
that stomped with great big lol'ping strides.
I thought at least we'd get something
that seemed a little dog-like,
not all squashed up, wheezing, frog-like,
with an ugly mug that's cross-eyed.
When it came the time to choose a dog, a pug was just the wrong type.

For a start, I checked online.
Turns out there are tons of sites that say, 'a pug is not a proper dog'.
Due to over-zealous breeding
they have problems with their breathing;
they're pretty much always sneezing;
apart from objects here and here, they struggle just to see things.
So for that and tons of reasons, I figured pugs were off the table.
Until we went to see one.

And she was pretty cute.

So we did something pretty stupid, right?
We called her Boo and took her home.
She's now my dog. I've been pleased to note
that she is capable of doggy things.
I've witnessed her both lick and sniff.
The dining room has lots of stains from all the times she's pissed on it.
She farts, she poos, she nibbles things,
she chews her way through everything.
She sleeps most days, her snoring grates;
she even snores when she's awake,
like the noise I think Darth Vader'd make
if he ran every leg of a relay race.
I'm the first to say she's pretty strange
but I also think she's pretty great.

And I took her out the other day to the local pub
where everybody loves her.
And one by one the regulars all make a massive fuss of her,
and she's wagging to the point that her bum could nearly wander off.
'Til one guy at the bar shouts over, starts mouthing off.
'Oi, mate! That ain't a proper dog, that's a rat you've got.
Be careful you don't trip on it!'
I hear that every now and then, and every time I grin a bit.
'Cause it's the same routine that follows:
she'll wag and run up to his chair and he'll scowl from high above her,
say her form just isn't proper,
'til eventually he's fussing her and then totally in love with her.

I don't care about his opinion, or that she changes his perspective.
What I care about and love is that I think Boo's really quite impressive.
Yeah, so her bark is more of a cough
and she's lopsided when she walks,
and she can't fetch a stick unless the stick is really small,
and he doesn't even know about her fear of basketballs.
But what's proper great about my dog is she doesn't care at all.

She's happy and she's loving and she thinks that she is great,
and I know there have been times when I didn't feel the same.
Because I've been in places where I've been told
that I'm not a proper poet,
and it hurt.
I stopped producing work, like they'd found my art's Achilles.
But since Boo's arrived, I'm like, 'Screw those guys.'
The labels all seem silly.

'Cause yeah, proper poets, proper dogs,
I've pictured it, don't want it much.
It reeks of class, and not of love.
Just lonely labels, stuffy stuff that's really dull and cumbersome.
It's fine for some but it's just not us.
We're Boo and Mark,
we're poet and dog.
Perhaps we're not the proper ones,
but you can't deny
that we shit and write in the same field as all the other ones.

So I'm dead happy with my puppy.
There's no way that I'd swap her,
just 'cause some self-professed expert
says there's dogs that are more proper.

I don't want another version.
She's something I take delight in,
and if I ever met a proper person
I don't think that I'd like 'em.

THE BOARD GAMES RAP

This is a safety announcement
for all the rappers in the building.
Particularly you grimers,
you angry little rhymers
using crappy one-liners
to hint your life is violence.
The truth is at the weekend you're all youth work providers,
off-duty Power Rangers; generous but spineless.
Think you're a threat to me?
No way do I buy this.
Forget that fake image you're relaying
and those fake words you keep on saying;
you're not dangerous.
But I am
whenever playing
board games.

Because you boys in the hood think you're up to no good
but your skills with a dice are lame
I'll top trump you weak punks,
you'll get trashed in Kerplunk
because I'm really, really, really, really good at board games.

I'm like an MB innovation,
rolling dice and dishing cards without any reservation.
When it comes to Risk I tell you this:
I am the global nation
coming atcha through Kamchatka
like a cannon infestation,
a Stone Age deforestation.
I give Mouse Trap demonstrations
and every game of Operation
is like a military... operation.
You'll soon make the observation
there's nothing trivial in my pursuit,
cracking skulls every evening
when I'm out of this suit.
Playing the odds on Pirate's Cove,
stealing your booty.
I did pretty well on Atmosfear
though that DVD was spooky.

I don't give a toss about a loss
against you in Call of Duty
'cause I disembowelled you in Guess Who
when I was Sue and you were James.
That's 'cause I'm really, really, really, really good at board games.

If it's Punch-Out I'll split your lip.
If it's poker I'll take each chip.
Buckaroo, I'll make you make him kick,
then lightning quick you'll find
that I've sunk your battleship.
I fry bacon when I play Pass the Pigs
'til you wee wee wee all the way home
and my meeple are lethal in every game of Carcassonne.
I'm in the zone in Monopoly,
just no stopping me,
hopping over pieces with that
little silver doggie,
snapping up the oranges. You're stuck on crap property
on Mayfair again? What will you offer me?

'Cause you guys think you're tight, think you're up for a fight
but you clearly aren't prepared for the pain.
I'll dice you up...
as long as it ain't a school night.
I'm really, really, really, really good at board games.

I'm better than good, I'm...

Very good.

Trained since the cradle
to dominate any kitchen table.
In Settlers of Catan I get more ore than Castle Grayskull
while you just get the sheep, which are cheap
and your bartering's pretty painful.
You wanna roleplay? Yeah, I dabble
but would rather take you out
in a game of Scrabble,
waving triple word scores

like they were lethal short swords,
spitting fire on to the board
so second place is your reward.

Because the boys in the hood think they're up to no good
but winners live forever and no one will remember any of your fakey rap names,
and I'll probably get the crap kicked out of me tonight
but I'm still really, really, really, really good at board games.

THE HOTTEST OF ALL OF THE GINGERS

Aristotle said redheads were emotionally unhousebroken.
They've always been thought to be somewhat outspoken.
The Greeks would even chop off scarlet heads
for fear they became vampires once they were dead.
A lot is said about redheads that's totally nonsense
designed to make you feel that your hair is a hindrance.
I'm here to say that's stupid, you're certainly no minger.
In fact you are the hottest of all of the gingers.

You can say what you like, but my passion's indignant.
I long for that skin with that little less pigment.
Coils of red springs tucked back behind ears.
Get back, Roman hordes; give me Boadicea!
Oh! handling men's hearts like a fireball with teeth,
so much red on that head and still red down beneath,
and even when munching on pancakes from Findus,
you are the hottest of all of the gingers.

Your hairdo resembles a blaze above porcelain.
Each flick of red tip I find totally awesome.
When it comes to your roots, be proud, don't regret it,
'cause studies have proved you need more anaesthetic.
Power and beauty both live in your blood,
plus it's easy to spot you late night in a club.
Even more rare than that list that was Schindler's,
you are the hottest of all of the gingers.

Springsteen claimed it took a redhead to get a dirty job done.
Well, this world's pretty grubby so we need more than one.
Don't be boorish, they're moreish, come bring on a truckful!
We'll accept that it means we get stuck with Mick Hucknall.
It's a small price to pay for hair so fresh-branded.
I'm not alone in wanting to be caught out red-handed.
I'll munch on red cinders when I'm into cunnilingus,
'cause you are the hottest of all of the gingers.

So get back all you girls in your summery thongs,
unless the curlies emerging are strawberry blonde.
I'm sure blondes and brunettes have a great deal of fun,
they don't need an umbrella when they go out in the sun,
but we'd stay inside 'til we've both had our full,
that thatch on your snatch a red rag to a bull,
and when we're done and you're gone, the thought of you lingers.
Because you are the hottest of all of the gingers.

ALL APOLOGIES

In the departure lounge
looking for our gate
we hear a man,
a slick,
blond-haired
well-dressed
man,
losing it.
'For goodness' sake!'
he booms,
his business suit
stretched
against waving arms.
He yells at his
four-year-old
son,
'Stop apologising!'
then yanks the child's hand
off his trouser leg
and stomps several feet away.

His wife, made up
in her red patterned dress,
kneels down to the boy.
'Daddy is angry
because you only
needed to say sorry once.'
The man turns, snaps,
'You didn't need to say sorry at all!'
There are tears from the boy
as his mother wipes his cheeks.
She is whispering
too softly for us to hear.
He tugs at his fluffy
blond hair
in gulped desperation
for the right thing
to say.

We keep walking but I'm
aching, I think
to apologise to someone.
Anyone, really.

IT'S STILL A FUCKING POEM

If it talks of things you don't believe in,
it's still a fucking poem.
If the metre isn't even,
it's still a fucking poem.
If it isn't all that intricate,
it's still a fucking poem.
If you don't feel all that into it,
it's still a fucking poem.

If it's popular, too jocular,
the rhyme scheme gets on top of ya,
if the metaphors are propping up
an argument that's rotten,
if it's written by some children,
it's still a fucking poem.
Graffitied to a building,
it's still a fucking poem.
Scribbled at a workshop,
it's still a fucking poem.
Or by someone you've not heard of,
it's still a fucking poem.

If it won all the awards,
if it leaves you feeling bored,
if it's half as good as yours,
it's still a fucking poem.

If it isn't asking questions,
isn't quite an argument,
it isn't all that liberal,
it's not attacking Parliament,
if the title has a footnote,
if the ending sort of spirals out,
if it will not be remembered by the world
a hundred years from now,

it's still a fucking poem, right?
It's still a fucking poem.
Still as much a poem as any piece you know of.

And it's not how you would write it,
but it's still a fucking poem.
You don't think that you like it,
but it's still a fucking poem.
And you can cry that it's appalling,
but it's still a fucking poem
and you aren't all that important, right?
you're not a fucking poem.

You're just a fucking poet stuffed
with too much guff from poems; just
leave it to the rest of us,
or go and write a poem.

THANKS & ACKNOWLEDGMENTS

Firstly, a huge thank you to Clive Birnie and everyone at Burning Eye Books for making all of this possible in the first place. It's an honour to get to work with such an exciting publisher and such a great bunch of people. Thanks for helping me to give it a shot!

Five years ago I wasn't sure that this was a real job. I still don't know whether it is or not, but I do know that if it weren't for the support of my friends and family I wouldn't be able to do this. Every cooked dinner, sofa to sleep on and sympathetic pint/chat has really helped me to keep going. Thank you all so much.

Thank you Mr Harvey for lending me your book of performance poems when I was 16. Thank you Ms Thompson for kicking my ass as much as you did and thank you Mr Martin for being an all-round inspiration.

Thanks to Thommie Gillow and Harriet Evans for their incredible patience in helping me to edit this collection and to Jacquelyn Williams and Jenni Bannister for all their help with proof reading – it would have been a very different (as in much worse) book without your advice!

Props to Mixy for teaching me more about words than many academics.

A massive shout out to Guy for his illustrations, especially the one for Ogre which was our first collaboration. Here's to many more!

Cheers to Boo for chewing through my laptop cable (twice) and for demanding to sit on my lap as I wrote this; as a result most of this was typed with one hand.

Lastly, (but not leastly) I must say thank you to my wonderful wife, Lucy. Thank you! You put up with me more than anyone else has to – every day I think about how lucky I am to have you. x